*Did*

# IPSWICH

## A MISCELLANY

Compiled by Julia Skinner
With particular reference to the work of Clive Tully

# THE FRANCIS FRITH COLLECTION

www.francisfrith.com

Based on a book first published in the United Kingdom in 2006 by The Francis Frith Collection®

This edition published exclusively for Oakridge in 2009 ISBN 978-1-84589-428-3

Text and Design copyright The Francis Frith Collection®
Photographs copyright The Francis Frith Collection® except where indicated.

The Frith® photographs and the Frith® logo are reproduced under licence from
Heritage Photographic Resources Ltd, the owners of the Frith® archive and trademarks.
'The Francis Frith Collection', 'Francis Frith' and 'Frith' are registered trademarks of
Heritage Photographic Resources Ltd.

British Library Cataloguing in Publication Data

Did You Know? Ipswich - A Miscellany
Compiled by Julia Skinner
With particular reference to the work of Clive Tully

The Francis Frith Collection
Frith's Barn, Teffont,
Salisbury, Wiltshire SP3 5QP
Tel: +44 (0) 1722 716 376
Email: info@francisfrith.co.uk
www.francisfrith.com

Printed and bound in Singapore

Front Cover: **IPSWICH, BUTTERMARKET 1893** 32204p

*The colour-tinting is for illustrative purposes only, and is not intended to be historically accurate*

AS WITH ANY HISTORICAL DATABASE, THE FRANCIS FRITH ARCHIVE IS CONSTANTLY BEING
CORRECTED AND IMPROVED, AND THE PUBLISHERS WOULD WELCOME INFORMATION ON
OMISSIONS OR INACCURACIES

# CONTENTS

# INTRODUCTION

Ipswich has been an important port for many centuries. It is situated at the point where the freshwater River Gipping joins the head of the tidal Orwell estuary, and even as far back as the 7th century Ipswich was the biggest port in the country, although at this period in history it suffered many Viking raids. It very quickly established itself as a place of industry, producing a distinctive grey type of pottery which was widely distributed, both throughout East Anglia and beyond. It is very likely that the close proximity of the East Anglian royal palace at Rendlesham had a marked bearing on the fortunes of the town, as much trade in imported fine wines, furs and textiles passed through here, as well as the products of the local industries being sent from here to other ports along the coast.

King John granted the town its first charter c1200, and throughout the Middle Ages the town prospered through the East Anglian wool trade. By the 17th century there was also a thriving shipbuilding industry using Suffolk oak, with shipyards lining the banks of the Orwell. In Georgian times the town suffered a commercial decline, but its prosperity was restored by the Industrial Revolution, evidenced by the large number of 19th-century houses in the town. Engineering businesses like Ransomes were established, producing everything from railway equipment to agricultural machinery. The construction of the revolutionary Wet Dock between 1839-42 improved the facilities that Ipswich could offer, and by the end of the First World War the port had expanded even more - the river had been dredged and quays built to accommodate large ships.

Today, despite the presence of the two major ports of Harwich and Felixstowe only ten miles away at the mouth of the Orwell,

Ipswich remains an important industrial and commercial centre. Ships still unload in the Wet Dock, but increasingly it is being taken over by yachts and pleasure boats, while cargo vessels unload at the riverside quays - the oil and grain terminals on the east bank, and the container and roll-on roll-off berths on the west.

The story of Ipswich is full of colourful characters and events, of which this book can only provide a brief glimpse.

**THE LOCK GATES 1921** 70413

# SUFFOLK DIALECT WORDS AND PHRASES

**'Ipsitch'** - thought by some to be the correct pronunciation of Ipswich.

**'Airy-wiggle'** - an earwig.

**'Hoistes'** - trousers that are too short.

**'Rabbitin on like the brook'** - talking too much.

**'Lummox'** - a clumsy person.

**'Shew'** - showed.

**'Coupla three'** - two or three.

**'Arter'** - after.

**'It's on the huh'** - it's not straight.

**'Biddy'** - old woman, widow.

**'Dwile'** - cloth (from the Dutch word 'dweil').

**'Mawther'** - a young girl.

**'Wholly'** - very.

# HAUNTED IPSWICH

Gippeswyk Hall is said to be haunted by a White Lady; she has been seen in the upper part of the hall on nights of the full moon.

The Woolpack Inn in Tuddenham Road has been declared to be the most haunted pub in the country by the Suffolk clairvoyant Sue Knock. She was contacted when a chef in the pub was terrified by an apparition which seemed to rush through his bedroom, and although he did not give her any descriptive details until after her investigation, she saw exactly the same spectre when she entered the room. She described it as a crouched, grey figure that disappeared into a wall. Later research found that the bedroom is next to a priest-hole, where Roman Catholic priests would hide during the days of persecution in the 16th century. Other ghosts said to haunt the inn are a pony-tailed sailor, an ex-landlord called George, and Admiral Vernon, who was MP for Ipswich from 1741 to 1754 - his ghost was once named Fred by locals in the past.

Paddy McGinty's pub is said to be haunted by the ghost of a monk who was murdered and thrown down a well at Holy Trinity Priory, which once stood on the site of Christchurch Mansion.

During the First World War, Ipswich was hit by a bomb dropped from a Zeppelin airship. The bomb killed a man in the house next door to the Bull Inn, Quay Street, and sightings of his ghost have been reported near the inn.

# IPSWICH MISCELLANY

The Wolsey Gate is the only surviving part of Cardinal Wolsey's ambitious plan to build a College of Cardinals in Ipswich. The building was started in 1527, and would have been quite extensive. Unfortunately, Wolsey fell from grace when he failed to expedite Henry VIII's divorce from Katherine of Aragon so that the king could marry Anne Boleyn, and it was never completed. The brick gateway seen in the photograph opposite, with its barely discernable royal cipher, is all that remains.

Cornhill, with its flamboyant mock Italian and Jacobean-style buildings, is on the original site of the market place of the town, but in less happy times it was also the place where several religious 'heretics' were burned at the stake. In February 1556, during the reign of Queen Mary, Joan Trunchfield, a shoe-maker's wife, and Anne Potton, a beer-maker's wife, were both burned to death here for their Protestant beliefs.

Christchurch Mansion was given to the town by F T Cobbold, a local banker. One of the Cobbold family was the clergyman-novelist Richard Cobbold, rector of Wortham in north Suffolk. His book 'Margaret Catchpole' was based on a true story of one of the Cobbold family's servant girls in the 18th century, who became involved with a local smuggler and ended up being transported to Australia.

In AD991, 93 Viking dragon ships carrying approximately 3,000 men sailed up the river to sack and pillage Ipswich. The force was led by the Norwegian commander Olaf Tryggvasson. After the attack on Ipswich, the Viking army headed for the Blackwater River estuary and landed on Northey Island, east of Maldon. The ensuing conflict was commemorated in the Anglo-Saxon poem 'The Battle of Maldon'.

**THE ANCIENT HOUSE 1921** 70398

Without doubt the best known building in Ipswich is the Ancient House (or Sparrowe's House), with its incredible plasterwork - an interesting feature is St George slaying a dragon whilst wearing a top hat. The first floor has oriel windows, in the centre of which are the arms of Charles II. It was around 1670 that Robert Sparrowe remodelled the building, with the pargetting reflecting his interest in the known world at that time - the plasterwork under each window represents Europe, Asia, Africa and America, the latter with a tobacco pipe. Europe is represented by an elegant lady with an open book; another lady under a palm tree is Asia; a naked man on a tree stump is Africa, and America is a nearly naked man in a feather head-dress.

The railway arrived in Ipswich in 1846, bringing with it opportunities for further expansion and improvements in the town's prosperity. A tunnel was cut through Stoke Hill enabling a line to run to Bury St Edmunds and in later years a line to Norwich was opened.

Ipswich, at the head of the Orwell Estuary, has been a major port for centuries. When photograph 32208 was taken (below), the port was starting to enjoy commercial success again after a long period of decline.

**THE DOCKS 1893** 32208

**THE PROMENADE 1893** 32210

**THE BUTTERMARKET 1921** 70404

Up until 1810, Ipswich's Buttermarket was indeed the scene for the sale of butter and other products. At the time that photograph 70404 was taken (above), it was one of the main shopping streets in the town.

The Unitarian Meeting House in Ipswich was built about 1700. Inside, four great wooden pillars, said to be from ships' masts, form part of the structure, while the carved pulpit is possibly the work of Grinling Gibbons.

The first trolley-buses began running in Ipswich in 1923, and services continued until 1963.

Christchurch Mansion was built by Edmund Withypoll in 1548-50 of red brick, on the site of Holy Trinity Priory. In 1893 the house and park were offered for sale. The house was purchased and given to the town in 1895 by Felix Cobbold, on condition that the Corporation bought the park. The house became a museum, and the park and the arboretum a pleasure ground. A monument to Queen Victoria stands in the park (photograph 70405, below).

**CHRISTCHURCH PARK 1921** 70405

At the end of the 18th century, Ipswich's most pressing problem was with the docks, where large ships were unable to berth. The river was silting up, and even at high tide it was becoming impossible to get upstream. The solution was to construct the Wet Dock by isolating a bend in the river and diverting the river itself into a bypass channel known as the New Cut. With lock gates to control access to it, the Wet Dock provided the means for ships to be able to dock at any state of the tide. The Wet Dock was constructed between 1839 and 1842, and at the time it was the largest such enclosed area of water in Europe.

The medieval church of St Mary le Tower (photograph 70402, opposite), for many years Ipswich's principal parish church, gave its name to Tower Street. The original spire collapsed in 1661, victim of a hurricane which swept across the town.

Early in the 19th century a Suffolk 'wise man' known as Old Winter is said to have practised white magic at Ipswich. He probably possessed hypnotic powers, which he used for punishing wrongdoers. Once he caught a man stealing vegetables from a doctor's garden, and bewitched him into sitting all night in the cabbage patch. On another occasion he is said to have compelled a thief to walk in circles for hours on end, carrying the load of firewood he had stolen.

Ipswich hit the headlines on 27 October 1936, when Wallis Simpson gained her divorce from Mr Simpson at the Ipswich Assizes. Edward VIII abdicated his throne to marry her, and the couple lived the rest of their lives in exile abroad, as the Duke and Duchess of Windsor.

ST MARY LE TOWER 1921 70402

**THE DOCKS c1955** I18049

East Anglia has a long tradition of growing malting barley, and Ipswich had a number of maltings. R & W Paul's was right on the dockside, and can be seen in photograph I18049, above.

The family of Geoffrey Chaucer, author of 'The Canterbury Tales', can be traced back four generations to Robert le Taverner of Ipswich, who died about 1280. In 1324, Geoffrey's father John (as a twelve-year-old boy) was kidnapped by an aunt in the hope of marrying him to her daughter, in an attempt to keep family property in Ipswich.

Ipswich Centre contains an all-glass building properly called the Willis Building, but often referred to as the 'Willis-Faber building' by locals. It dates from 1974, and was designed by Norman Foster. It became the youngest Grade I listed building in Britain in 1991.

Paddle steamers like the SS 'Norfolk', seen in photograph 51246, below, used to operate along the East Coast, running pleasure trips to places like Felixstowe and Harwich. In the background of the photograph are the masts of cargo ships.

**THE RIVER ORWELL AND SS 'NORFOLK' 1904** 51246

**BUTTERMARKET 1893** 32204

GOOD
CHEAP
STATIONERY.

GOOD
CHEAP
STATIONERY

PRINTING
BOOKBINDING

19

FRESTON TOWER
**1893** 32233

From 1611 to 1634 Ipswich was a major centre for emigration to New England. This was organised by the Town Lecturer, Samuel Ward, whose brother Nathaniel Ward was the first minister of Ipswich, Massachusetts. A 17th-century portrait of Samuel Ward can be seen in Christchurch Mansion. A plaque on Christ Church in Tacket Street commemorates Rev William Gordon who went to America; he worked for George Washington, and wrote the first account of the American Revolution in 1788.

Coastal Suffolk might not be the first place you would think of for a skyscraper, but the charming Tudor redbrick folly of Freston Tower (see photograph opposite) could fit the bill, albeit in a scaled-down manner. It was probably built by a prominent Ipswich merchant, Thomas Gooding, around 1550 as a study for his daughter.

Ransomes, Sims and Jeffries Engineers of Ipswich were in their day a major British agricultural machinery maker, famous for traction engines, ploughs and other tilling equipment. The company (as Ransomes) was founded in 1789 by Robert Ransome, an ironfounder who moved to Ipswich from Norwich. In 1989 the whole of the agricultural implement business was sold to Electrolux, leaving Ransomes solely as a manufacturer of lawn mowers, making the Westwood and Mountfield mower brands. The company was taken over by Textron Inc, USA and their independent existence ended early in 1998.

There was a sugar beet factory at Ipswich for many years, which serviced 787 growers, who produced 800,000 tonnes of beet each year. The factory was closed in 2001.

In medieval times Ipswich was famous for its shrine to Our Lady of Ipswich (also known as Our Lady of Grace). It was positioned just outside the west gate of the town wall, and the site is now marked by a plaque. It was a very popular destination for pilgrimages - only the shrine at Walsingham in Norfolk attracted more visitors. The shrine was suppressed during the Reformation of the 16th century, and its famous statue of the Virgin Mary was taken to Chelsea to be burnt. Although documents confirm that the statue did arrive at Chelsea, there are no reliable records to confirm that it was destroyed. Intriguingly, a wooden statue of the Madonna and Child in a church in the Italian seaside town of Nettuno may well be the one that used to grace Ipswich's shrine. It matches contemporary descriptions of the Suffolk statue, and there is evidence in Nettuno archives that the statue originally came from Ipswich. Although the statue has been altered, artistic details suggest that it is English. The statue is known in Nettuno as 'Our Lady of the Graces' or 'The English Lady'. A Latin inscription was found on its back which translates as the Marian phrase 'Thou art gracious'. Ipswich is known to have been the only Marian shrine in England dedicated to Our Lady of Grace. There are two theories as to how the statue may have reached Italy. One theory is that it was sold by an English official instead of being burnt, the other is that the statue may have been rescued by English sailors before it could be burnt, and smuggled on board a ship. Perhaps it came to Nettuno as part of a shipwreck, or was given by sailors as a donation for safe refuge from a storm. A replica of the statue now stands in Lady Lane in Ipswich town centre.

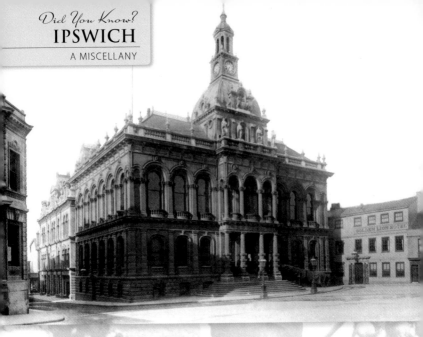

**THE TOWN HALL 1896** 37308

The Italianate Town Hall was erected in 1867. The four figures below the clock represent Commerce, Agriculture, Learning and Justice.

The Ipswich Hoard of five Iron Age gold torcs, dating from around 75BC, was found during construction work in Ipswich in 1968; a sixth torc was found the following year. Torcs are heavy ornaments worn around the neck, made by twisting two rods of gold around each other. Scientific analysis has shown that the Ipswich torcs are made from an alloy of 90% gold and 10% silver. The Ipswich Hoard is one of Britain's most important Iron Age discoveries, and can be seen in the British Museum.

The painters John Constable and Thomas Gainsborough lived and worked in Ipswich. The art gallery adjoining Christchurch Mansion houses a fine collection of paintings by both artists.

Dating from the 15th century, St Margaret's Church is regarded as the finest church in Ipswich (photograph 32220, below). The exterior is richly decorated with stone and flint, while inside stands a monument to Sir Edmund Withipool, who built nearby Christchurch Mansion.

**ST MARGARET'S CHURCH 1893** 32220

**TAVERN STREET 1896** 37306

**THE DOCKS 1921** 70412

Photograph 70412 (above) shows the view across the Entrance Lock towards Cliff Brewery, behind the trees, with Cliff Quay to the right. The eight spritsail barges wait to bring their cargoes into the dock. Spritsails were the last working barges in northern Europe, continuing until the early 1960s. The main cargoes brought into Ipswich were grain, barley, coal and timber.

When Daniel Defoe visited Ipswich in 1722, he commented on how many townsfolk used Christchurch Park, likening its popularity to that of Kensington Gardens.

At one time Ipswich had a small grass-runway airport, which ran regular flights to the Netherlands. The area has now been redeveloped into the new residential district of Ravenswood.

Sailing barges are seen in photograph 70411 (below) tied up in the Wet Dock, the non-tidal part of the port of Ipswich. Adjacent to the dock are large warehouses, including that of Cranfields who, along with Pauls, owned their own large fleets of barges. Outside the Wet Dock, tidal moorings were built for larger ships.

**ST PETER'S DOCK 1921** 70411

**TAVERN STREET c1955** I18036

Tavern Street contains the Great White Horse Hotel which, despite its Georgian façade, is a timber-framed building dating back to the 16th-century (seen on the right-hand side of photograph I18036, above). Famous visitors have included Charles Dickens, who wrote about it in 'The Pickwick Papers', George II (1736), Louis XVIII of France (1807), and Lord Nelson (1800).

The story of how Silent Street got its name is one of the more tragic episodes in the history of Ipswich. All the inhabitants of the street died in the same outbreak of the plague, after which the street became sadly 'silent'.

Katherine of Aragon, first wife of Henry VIII, came to the shrine of Our Lady of Grace in Ipswich several times in 1517 to pray for a son - unsuccessfully, as it turned out.

On the corner where St Nicholas Street is joined by Silent Street stands a magnificent group of Tudor houses with a carved corner post (photograph I18047, below). Cardinal Wolsey is reputed to have been born in this area in about 1475, and a plaque on one of the houses commemorates this.

**SILENT STREET, WOLSEY'S BIRTHPLACE c1955** I18047

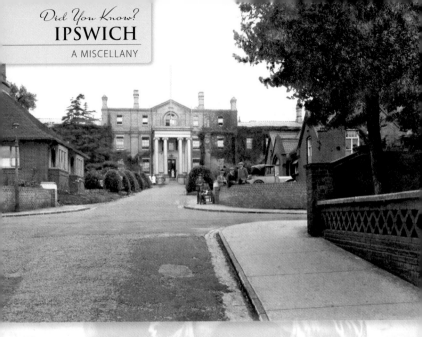

**THE HOSPITAL 1921** 70406

The East Suffolk Hospital was founded in 1835, starting out as a two-storey building. It was extended upwards in 1869, and a children's wing was added some five years later (photograph 70406, above).

The Ipswich Transport Museum is unique in that it has the largest collection of transport items in Britain devoted to just one town. Everything in the museum was either made or used in and around Ipswich. The collection has been building up since about 1965, and moved to its current home in part of the former Priory Heath Trolleybus Depot in 1988. The Museum also organises the annual Ipswich to Felixstowe historic vehicle road run, which takes place every May.

The designer of Nelson's 'Victory', Thomas Slade, is buried in the graveyard of St Clement's, otherwise known as the Sailors' Church, in Ipswich.

The earlier Corn Exchange on Cornhill was demolished in 1880 for the new Post Office. The replacement was built in 1882 in a mixture of Italianate styles, with French pavilions on the roof (32203, above). The front towards King Street had shops on the ground floor, one of which was the Essex and Suffolk Fire Office. The building became a film theatre in 1973.

**THE CORN EXCHANGE 1893** 32203

**FORE STREET 1893** 32206

**THE DOCKS 1921** 70415

Ransome and Rapier was a successful local engineering firm, which was created when Ransomes split. They concentrated on heavy machinery, such as cranes, instead of garden and agricultural machines, and among their impressive list of achievements were the first railway in China, the Aswan high dam in Egypt and the turntable for the revolving restaurant at the Post Office Tower in London. The company was taken over by Robert Maxwell, and closed in 1988.

Ipswich still has 12 medieval churches in the town centre, but only six of them still function as places of worship. St Stephen's is now serving as the Tourist Office.

The history of Ipswich is well illustrated at the Ipswich Museum, where the collection includes Saxon weapons and jewellery, and information about the Mildenhall and Sutton Hoo treasures (see also page 40).

The basic street pattern of the town centre is still that of the medieval town, including a fine range of buildings dating from the 15th century onwards. Like Norwich, Ipswich was once surrounded by a defensive wall, a legacy of which can be found in many of the street names, such as Westgate and Northgate. The actual West Gate was demolished in 1781.

**ELECTRIC HOUSE AND THE CAR PARK c1955** I18044

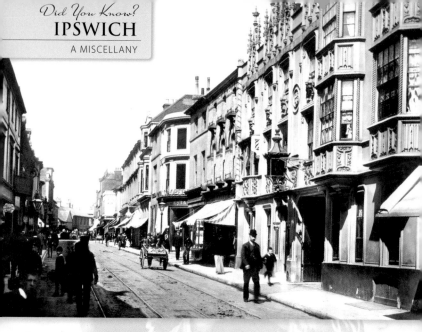

**WESTGATE STREET 1893** 32200

In 1614, Ipswich was quoted as having more shipwrights than any port in England.

Hidden beneath a Suffolk school playground, among quiet residential streets, is the Clifford Road Air Raid Shelter Museum. The air raid shelter was sealed up after the Second World War and forgotten, but was discovered when workmen in 1989 found one of the entrances. The shelter was found to be in excellent condition, and in its new role provides a fascinating picture of life on the home front during the Second World War. Full of wartime memorabilia, the museum is open to visitors on certain days in the summer.

No English town has been lived in by English speaking inhabitants for a longer continuous period than Ipswich - although Colchester has been inhabited for a longer length of time, that includes a period of Roman occupation when the locals presumably spoke Latin or a Celtic language.

Sir Alf Ramsay, the manager who took England to World Cup football victory in 1966, was also a one-time manager of Ipswich Town FC. Sir Alf lived and died in Ipswich, and a statue of him stands opposite the ITFC stadium in Portman Road.

**THE TOWN HALL AND THE POST OFFICE 1896** 37307

Nine miles north-east of Ipswich is Sutton Hoo, the site of the famous ship burial which was excavated in 1939, in an area of 18 burial mounds. Beneath the largest mound were the remains of a 30ft oak ship. As no body was found at the time of the excavation it was assumed that it was an 'empty' burial, but recent research shows that there may originally have been a body, which was completely destroyed by the acid soil. The ship was found to be full of objects, or grave goods, many of which were

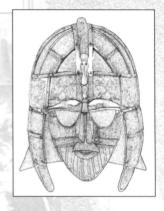

**AN ARTIST'S IMPRESSION OF THE SUTTON HOO HELMET** F6024

made of gold and silver, which are now on display in the British museum. They included weapons, coins, armour and cups as well as garments and textiles, of the finest craftsmanship. The opulence and value of these objects signifies a grave of someone of the greatest importance, certainly someone from the Wuffings royal family which settled in East Anglia from Sweden in the late 5th century. However the identity of the occupant remains one of archaeology's great discussion points. The dates of the coins found in the grave range between AD575 and AD620. Four major East Anglian kings are known to have ruled around this time - Raedwald, Eorpwald, Sigebert and Ecric - and Raedwald is thought to have been the most likely candidate. The famous Sutton Hoo helmet has been replicated in this drawing from fragments found in the ship burial. The original was made of gilded bronze, and can be seen in the British Museum.

In St Clement's churchyard is the grave of John Woolward, who was killed after being struck by lightning.

# SPORTING IPSWICH

Ipswich Town Football Club's record victory and defeat happened just 15 months apart: a 10-0 victory over Floriana in a European match in September 1962 was followed by a 10-1 defeat by Fulham on Boxing Day 1963.

Speedway has a long and proud tradition in Ipswich, dating back to the very first meeting at Portman Road in 1950, and covering two incarnations of the Foxhall Stadium. The Witches' finest year though was surely 1998. The team won the Elite League by a massive 17 points, as well as the Knockout Cup and the Craven Shield. The strength of the team was such that three riders won individual championships, Tony Rickardsson (the World Championship), Chris Louis (the British Championship) and Scott Nicholls (the British under-21 title).

Ipswich and East Suffolk Cricket Club was founded in 1853, and has existed ever since, although from 1936 to 1951 the club survived with no ground of its own. In 1936, Ipswich Town Football Club took over the Portman Road ground that both clubs shared, and the cricket team was unable to find a new home until it moved to Chantry Park in 1951.

Two managers of Ipswich Town Football Club have gone on to manage the England team. Alf Ramsay and Bobby Robson both had success at Ipswich Town FC, winning two major trophies each, before becoming England's two most successful managers. Sir Alf, of course, led England to their World Cup win of 1966, whilst Sir Bobby took England to the semi-final in 1990.

# QUIZ QUESTIONS

Answers on page 49.

1. What was the Anglo-Saxon name for Ipswich?

2. Who hid in the Attic Room of the Ancient House?

3. What do the four statues on the Post Office on Cornhill represent?

4. Which important post in Ipswich was held by Lord Nelson, who died at the battle of Trafalgar in 1805?

5. Who was 'Old Grog', and how did he get his name?

6. Which ancient emergency vehicle came to the rescue in the 21st century?

7. Which medieval author was rude about the merchants of Ipswich?

8. Which major continent is missing from the plasterwork decoration on the Ancient House, and why?

9. Which royal wedding took place in Ipswich in 1297?

10. What were Port Men?

**THE RIVER ORWELL 1921** 70414

# RECIPE

## IPSWICH ALMOND PUDDING

### Ingredients
450ml/15floz milk
150ml/5fl oz. double cream
50g/2oz fresh white
breadcrumbs
75g/3oz caster sugar

175g/6oz ground almonds
1 teaspoonful orange flower
or rose water (available from
chemists)
3 beaten eggs
25g/1oz butter

Place the milk and cream in a saucepan and heat until warmed. Place the breadcrumbs in a large mixing bowl, and pour the warm milk and cream over them. Mix in the sugar, almonds and orange or rose water and leave to soak for 15 minutes. Add the beaten eggs to the breadcrumb mixture and mix well. Pour the mixture into a buttered pie dish and dot the surface with small knobs of butter. Place the dish in a deep roasting tin with enough hot water to come half way up the sides of the pie dish. Bake in a preheated oven until set (180 degrees C, 350 degrees F, Gas Mark 4). Serve hot with cream or custard.

SUFFOLK GALLERY  TURNERS

WALLPAPERS  BRI

# RECIPE

## GOD'S KITCHEL CAKE

It was a particular Suffolk custom for children to visit their godparents at Christmas time and ask for their blessings.
A small cake called a God's kitchel was specially made for visiting godchildren. There was an old saying: 'Ask me a blessing and I will give you a kitchel', and in Chaucer's 'Canterbury Tales', written in 1386, we find the lines: 'Give us a bushel, wheat, malt or rye, A God's kitchel, or a trip of cheese.'

| *Ingredients* | |
|---|---|
| 450g/1lb made-up flaky pastry | 50g/2oz candied peel |
| | 75g/3oz sugar |
| 115g/4oz margarine | 50g/2oz ground almonds |
| 225g/8oz currants | 1 teaspoon powdered cinnamon |
| 25g/1oz sultanas | 1 teaspoon grated nutmeg |

Melt the margarine in a large saucepan. Add the dried fruit, peel, sugar, ground almonds and spices. Mix well. Halve the pastry and roll one piece across into a square about 30cm (12 inches) across - it should be rolled quite thin. Place it on a greased baking sheet. Moisten the edges of the rolled pastry with milk or water, and spread the filling on it, leaving an edge of about 1cm (half an inch). Cover with the second piece of pastry, rolled out to fit. Seal the edges well by pressing lightly together. Carefully mark the top of the cake with a knife into 6cm (2½ inch) squares, but without cutting through the pastry. Bake near the top of a preheated oven, 220 degrees C/425 degrees F/Gas Mark 7 until nicely golden brown. Sprinkle with caster sugar and leave to cool for a few minutes, then divide into sections and leave them to cool on a wire rack.

**ST STEPHEN'S CHURCH**
**1921** 70392

48

# QUIZ ANSWERS

1.  Gippeswic.

2.  Local tradition says that Charles II hid in the Attic Room of the Ancient House in the Buttermarket whilst escaping his pursuers after the battle of Worcester in 1651.

3.  The four statues on the Post Office represent Industry, Electricity, Steam and Commerce.

4.  Lord Nelson was High Steward of Ipswich in 1800.

5.  'Old Grog' was the nickname given to Admiral Vernon of the Royal Navy, who lived at Orwell Park at Nacton, just outside Ipswich, after the boat cloak that he wore, which was made out of a coarse fabric called grogram. In an attempt to decrease the number of drunken brawls on his ships, Admiral Vernon ordered that all rations of rum to sailors were to be watered down and provided no more than twice a day, six hours apart. The irate sailors named this diluted rum 'grog', after the Admiral. The custom of giving Royal Navy sailors their twice-daily ration of grog was only discontinued in 1970.

6.  An 1870 Merryweather Manual Fire Escape from the Transport Museum, which was recently used to help workmen paint street lamps.

7.  Geoffrey Chaucer satirised the merchants of Ipswich in 'The Canterbury Tales'.

8.  Australia - it had not been 'discovered' when the decoration was done in the 17th century!

9.  In 1297 the daughter of Edward I, Princess Elizabeth, married the Count of Holland in the shrine of Our Lady of Ipswich.

10. In medieval times Ipswich created Port Men instead of town burgesses, because its wealth was dependent upon the river. This tradition is remembered today in the name of the football stadium, Portman Road.

**THE GRAMMAR SCHOOL AND UPPER ARBORETUM 1921** 70396

# FRANCIS FRITH

## PIONEER VICTORIAN PHOTOGRAPHER

Francis Frith, founder of the world-famous photographic archive, was a complex and multi-talented man. A devout Quaker and a highly successful Victorian businessman, he was philosophical by nature and pioneering in outlook. By 1855 he had already established a wholesale grocery business in Liverpool, and sold it for the astonishing sum of £200,000, which is the equivalent today of over £15,000,000. Now in his thirties, and captivated by the new science of photography, Frith set out on a series of pioneering journeys up the Nile and to the Near East.

## INTRIGUE AND EXPLORATION

He was the first photographer to venture beyond the sixth cataract of the Nile. Africa was still the mysterious 'Dark Continent', and Stanley and Livingstone's historic meeting was a decade into the future. The conditions for picture taking confound belief. He laboured for hours in his wicker dark-room in the sweltering heat of the desert, while the volatile chemicals fizzed dangerously in their trays. Back in London he exhibited his photographs and was 'rapturously cheered' by members of the Royal Society. His reputation as a photographer was made overnight.

## VENTURE OF A LIFE-TIME

By the 1870s the railways had threaded their way across the country, and Bank Holidays and half-day Saturdays had been made obligatory by Act of Parliament. All of a sudden the working man and his family were able to enjoy days out, take holidays, and see a little more of the world.

With typical business acumen, Francis Frith foresaw that these new tourists would enjoy having souvenirs to commemorate their days out. For the next thirty years he travelled the country by train and by pony and trap, producing fine photographs of seaside resorts and beauty spots that were keenly bought by millions of Victorians. These prints were painstakingly pasted into family albums and pored over during the dark nights of winter, rekindling precious memories of summer excursions. Frith's studio was soon supplying retail shops all over the country, and by 1890 F Frith & Co had become the greatest specialist photographic publishing company in the world, with over 2,000 sales outlets, and pioneered the picture postcard.

## FRANCIS FRITH'S LEGACY

Francis Frith had died in 1898 at his villa in Cannes, his great project still growing. By 1970 the archive he created contained over a third of a million pictures showing 7,000 British towns and villages.

Frith's legacy to us today is of immense significance and value, for the magnificent archive of evocative photographs he created provides a unique record of change in the cities, towns and villages throughout Britain over a century and more. Frith and his fellow studio photographers revisited locations many times down the years to update their views, compiling for us an enthralling and colourful pageant of British life and character.

We are fortunate that Frith was dedicated to recording the minutiae of everyday life. For it is this sheer wealth of visual data, the painstaking chronicle of changes in dress, transport, street layouts, buildings, housing and landscape that captivates us so much today, offering us a powerful link with the past and with the lives of our ancestors.

Computers have now made it possible for Frith's many thousands of images to be accessed almost instantly. The archive offers every one of us an opportunity to examine the places where we and our families have lived and worked down the years. Its images, depicting our shared past, are now bringing pleasure and enlightenment to millions around the world a century and more after his death.

For further information visit: www.francisfrith.com

## INTERIOR DECORATION

Frith's photographs can be seen framed and as giant wall murals in thousands of pubs, restaurants, hotels, banks, retail stores and other public buildings throughout Britain. These provide interesting and attractive décor, generating strong local interest and acting as a powerful reminder of gentler days in our increasingly busy and frenetic world.

## FRITH PRODUCTS

All Frith photographs are available as prints and posters in a variety of different sizes and styles. In the UK we also offer a range of other gift and stationery products illustrated with Frith photographs, although many of these are not available for delivery outside the UK – see our web site for more information on the products available for delivery in your country.

## THE INTERNET

Over 100,000 photographs of Britain can be viewed and purchased on the Frith web site. The web site also includes memories and reminiscences contributed by our customers, who have personal knowledge of localities and of the people and properties depicted in Frith photographs. If you wish to learn more about a specific town or village you may find these reminiscences fascinating to browse. Why not add your own comments if you think they would be of interest to others? See **www.francisfrith.com**

## PLEASE HELP US BRING FRITH'S PHOTOGRAPHS TO LIFE

Our authors do their best to recount the history of the places they write about. They give insights into how particular towns and villages developed, they describe the architecture of streets and buildings, and they discuss the lives of famous people who lived there. But however knowledgeable our authors are, the story they tell is necessarily incomplete.

Frith's photographs are so much more than plain historical documents. They are living proofs of the flow of human life down the generations. They show real people at real moments in history; and each of those people is the son or daughter of someone, the brother or sister, aunt or uncle, grandfather or grandmother of someone else. All of them lived, worked and played in the streets depicted in Frith's photographs.

We would be grateful if you would give us your insights into the places shown in our photographs: the streets and buildings, the shops, businesses and industries. Post your memories of life in those streets on the Frith website: what it was like growing up there, who ran the local shop and what shopping was like years ago; if your workplace is shown tell us about your working day and what the building is used for now. Read other visitors' memories and reconnect with your shared local history and heritage. With your help more and more Frith photographs can be brought to life, and vital memories preserved for posterity, and for the benefit of historians in the future.

Wherever possible, we will try to include some of your comments in future editions of our books. Moreover, if you spot errors in dates, titles or other facts, please let us know, because our archive records are not always completely accurate—they rely on 140 years of human endeavour and hand-compiled records. You can email us using the contact form on the website.

Thank you!

For further information, trade, or author enquiries
please contact us at the address below:

**The Francis Frith Collection, Frith's Barn, Teffont,
Salisbury, Wiltshire, England SP3 5QP.**

Tel: +44 (0)1722 716 376  Fax: +44 (0)1722 716 881

e-mail: sales@francisfrith.co.uk  **www.francisfrith.com**